Countries Around the World

Portugal

Charlotte Guillain

Heinemann Library
Chicago, Illinois

www.capstonepub.com
Visit our website to find out more information about Heinemann-Raintree books.

To order:
☎ Phone 888-454-2279
▭ Visit www.capstonepub.com
to browse our catalog and order online.

Edited by Laura Knowles
Designed by Victoria Allen
Original illustrations © Capstone Global Library Ltd 2012
Illustrated by Oxford Designers and Illustrators
Picture research by Mica Brancic
Originated by Capstone Global Library
Printed and bound in China by CTPS

15 14 13 12 11
10 9 8 7 6 5 4 3 2 1

Library of Congress Cataloging-in-Publication Data
Guillain, Charlotte.
   Portugal / Charlotte Guillain.
      p. cm.—(Countries around the world)
   Includes bibliographical references and index.
   ISBN 978-1-4329-6109-1 (hb)—ISBN 978-1-4329-6135-0
(pb) 1. Portugal—Juvenile literature. I. Title.
DP517.G85 2012
946.9—dc22
                              2011015434

Acknowledgments
We would like to thank the following for permission to reproduce photographs: Corbis pp. **7** (© Hulton-Deutsch Collection), **10** (© Bettmann), **11** (© Bettmann), **12** (Sygma/ © Patrick Chauvel), **13** (© Bettmann), **22** (Reuters/© Victor Fraile), **34** (Robert Harding World Imagery/© Graham Lawrence); Getty Images pp. **8** (The Bridgeman Art Library), **27** (Bloomberg/Vanda De Mello), **29** (Bloomberg/Adam Berry), **30** (AFP Photo/Sebastien Feval); iStockphoto pp. **21** (© robert van beets), **33** (© Christian Martínez Kempin), **39** (© Mlenny Photography); Shutterstock pp. **5** (© André Viegas), **15** (© Ultimathule), **17** (© Carlos Caetano), **18** (© Inacio Pires), **20** (© Volodymyr Burdiak), **23** (© Dmitriy Yakovlev), **24** (© Christina Solodukhina), **25** (© Gary James Calder), **28** (© Filipe B. Varela), **35** (© Pedro Jorge Henriques Monteiro), **46** (© Christophe Testi).

Cover photograph of the beach of Paraiso in the tourist region of Algarve, Portugal, reproduced with permission of Shutterstock/© Inacio Pires.

We would like to thank Carla Vicencio Prior (www.cvp-research.co.uk) for her invaluable help in the preparation of this book.

Every effort has been made to contact copyright holders of material reproduced in this book. Any omissions will be rectified in subsequent printings if notice is given to the publisher.

Disclaimer
All the Internet addresses (URLs) given in this book were valid at the time of going to press. However, due to the dynamic nature of the Internet, some addresses may have changed, or sites may have changed or ceased to exist since publication. While the author and publisher regret any inconvenience this may cause readers, no responsibility for any such changes can be accepted by either the author or the publisher.

Contents

Some words are printed in bold, **like this**. You can find out what they mean by looking in the glossary.

Introducing Portugal

What do you know about Portugal? Perhaps you have watched the soccer team play or have heard of its capital, Lisbon. Have you ever eaten Portuguese food? You may have learned about this country in history lessons. Would you like to know more about the country's past, geography, **culture**, and people?

Small but mighty

Portugal is a small country in southwest Europe. The North Atlantic Ocean lies to the west, and Spain borders Portugal to the east. The country covers an area of 35,556 square miles (92,090 square kilometers), making it slightly smaller than the state of Indiana.

Centuries ago, Portugal was one of the world's most powerful countries, with land and influence all around the world. Located on the edge of Europe, Portugal was well situated in an age of seafaring to settle and trade in new lands. Although the country is no longer one of the most powerful in the world, the **legacy** of those wealthy times can still be seen in Portugal today.

A unique nation

You might expect Portugal to have been dominated by its huge neighbor, Spain. However, although Spain has occupied Portuguese lands at various points in history, Portugal has resisted Spanish domination and has its own unique culture, cuisine, and language. Portuguese people are very proud of their fascinating country.

How to say...

hello	*olá*	(o-LA)
goodbye	*adeus*	(a-DEOOSH)
how are you?	*como estás?*	(komo esh-TASH?)
yes	*sim*	(singh)
no	*não*	(na-UHM)
please	*por favor*	(por FA-vor)

Lisbon is Portugal's beautiful capital city.

History: Exploration and Occupation

Early humans were living in Portugal 30,000 years ago. **Neolithic** humans came to Portugal from southern Spain, bringing farming, pottery, and metal-working skills.

Settlers

Celts arrived in northern Portugal between 700 and 600 BCE. Meanwhile, Phoenicians from the area that is now Lebanon settled in coastal areas of Portugal, followed by **settlers** from modern-day Tunisia. From 210 BCE, Romans began to move into Portugal. Various **tribes** further inland resisted Roman invasion and held out for 50 years. Julius Caesar brought Portugal within the Roman **Empire**, and in 60 BCE a capital was established at Olisipo (Lisbon).

VIRIATHUS (DIED 139 BCE)

Viriathus was a warrior who led a tribe of Celts against the Romans. He stopped the Romans from advancing north in Portugal for 50 years. In the end the Romans bribed his own warriors to kill him as he slept. Without his strong opposition, the Romans were able to invade the rest of Portugal.

Visigoths invade

Christianity came to Portugal in the 1st century CE. Roman rule was declining by the begining of the 400s CE, and invading tribes such as the Suevi and Visigoths began to take land. The Visigoths ruled for over 200 years and were based in Spain.

The Moors in Portugal

Moors from North Africa then began to settle in the south of the country in the 8th century. The Moors were mainly **Muslim** but were tolerant of Christians and **Jews** and brought new technologies. However, Christians wanted to take the land back. They began fighting in Spain around 718 CE. This struggle, known as the *Reconquista*, continued for centuries. In 1139 Afonso Henriques declared himself the first king of Portugal. Only the regions of Alentejo and the Algarve remained under Muslim control. Finally Afonso III (1210–1279) took back these lands in 1249 and established Portugal much as it is today.

Afonso I was the first king of Portugal.

A stronger power

Afonso III's son, the skilled Dom Dinis (1279–1325), made Portugal stronger. He built **fortresses** along the Spanish border and improved farming and trade. Under his rule education and the arts flourished.

Looking overseas

During the 1400s the Portuguese began exploring the world, hoping to find wealth and spread Christianity. Portuguese explorers arrived in Madeira around 1419 and the Azores in 1427. By 1460 much of the west coast of Africa had been explored. Bartolomeu Dias sailed round the southern tip of Africa in 1488, and Vasco da Gama opened up the trade route to India a decade later. The Portuguese **monarchy** became the richest in Europe. The explorer Pedro Álvares Cabral arrived in Brazil in 1500, and by the mid-1500s, Portugal had trading posts at Goa, Malacca, Ormuz, and Macau.

Vasco da Gama (around 1460–1524) is one of Portugal's most famous explorers.

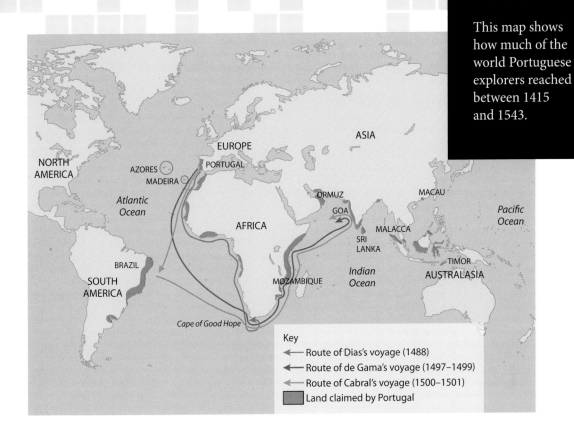

This map shows how much of the world Portuguese explorers reached between 1415 and 1543.

Key
← Route of Dias's voyage (1488)
← Route of de Gama's voyage (1497–1499)
← Route of Cabral's voyage (1500–1501)
Land claimed by Portugal

Spanish rule

In 1580, Philip II of Spain was crowned Filipe I of Portugal. Portugal's **identity** was largely protected and the **economy** improved, but the Portuguese people hated foreign rule. Portugal lost British and Dutch **allies** and trade links and started to lose parts of its overseas empire. Later, the Spanish **taxed** the Portuguese people heavily. In 1640, the Portuguese duke of Bragança was declared King João IV of Portugal. Spain was too busy with other wars to stop this from happening.

Daily life

While royalty, the upper class, and traders became very wealthy, the rest of the Portuguese population did not gain much from the new discoveries. Most of the riches from the "New World" went to the monarchy and were not **invested** in businesses at home.

Disaster and decline

In 1755, a huge earthquake destroyed the capital city of Lisbon. The tremors were followed by a devastating fire and a **tsunami**. The king's chief minister, the Marquês de Pombal, set about rebuilding the city and modernizing Portugal. However, as the country recovered, a new threat appeared. Portugal was pulled into war against the French leader Napoleon by its ally, Great Britain. In 1807 Napoleon invaded Portugal and was only defeated in 1811. Portugal was weakened and its richest overseas **colony**, Brazil, became **independent** in 1822.

The Lisbon earthquake killed 90,000 people, and the city was ruined.

Salazar

At the start of the 1900s, Portuguese industry was not growing, trade was limited, and many people **emigrated** to Brazil. Then in 1908 King Dom Carlos and his son were **assassinated** by people who wanted Portugal to become a **republic**. Portugal was declared a republic in 1910, and the remaining royal family fled the country. Chaos continued though, with 45 changes of government in 16 years.

In 1932, António de Oliveira Salazar became prime minister. Salazar would not give up Portugal's colonies in Africa and Asia, and this led to unpopular and expensive wars. Salazar died in 1970, and the overseas wars continued, along with new economic problems at home. In 1974 a relatively peaceful **coup** took place. It was called the Revolution of the Carnations because soldiers put flowers in their gun barrels. Portugal became a **democracy**.

Salazar established a very strict and controlling regime, where many who opposed the government were imprisoned and tortured.

New beginnings

By 1975 all of Portugal's African colonies were independent. Not long after it gained independence, **civil war** started in Angola. Nine days after East Timor in Southeast Asia became independent, Indonesia invaded. Many civilians were injured or killed. East Timor remained occupied for the next 24 years. Many **refugees** from former colonies came to Portugal to settle.

Fighting continued on and off in Angola until 2009.

It took several years for democracy to become established in Portugal. Mário Soares, the **socialist** leader, led the government until 1977. Following this, several **coalition** governments ruled one after the other. By the early 1980s, a more stable government was able to start modernizing the country, and Portugal joined the **European Union (EU)** (known then as the EEC).

Into the future

Although Portugal's economy grew during the 1980s, the country was affected by **strikes**. From 1992, Portugal was allowed to trade with the rest of the EU. This meant that the country faced new competition. The economy went into **recession**, and Portugal remained undeveloped compared to the rest of the EU.

In 2004, José Manuel Durão Barroso became the first Portuguese president of the **European Commission**. In the same year Portugal hosted the European Football (Soccer) Championships, raising the country's international profile further. The prime minister, José Sócrates, did much to improve technology and **infrastructure**, but Portugal's economy was in such a desperate state by 2011 that he was forced to resign.

MARIA DE LOURDES PINTASSILGO

(1930–2004)

Maria de Lourdes Pintassilgo was the first female prime minister in Portugal and only the second European woman to be a prime minister. She worked to improve women's rights and tried to bring religious and nonreligious groups together. She was only prime minister from 1979 to 1980, but she worked hard all her life to bring about positive change in her country.

Regions and Resources: From Mountains to Beaches

Portugal is one of Europe's smallest countries. The country's only border is with Spain, covering 754 miles (1,214 kilometers). The islands of Madeira and the Azores in the Atlantic Ocean are also Portuguese territories. Portugal's capital is Lisbon.

Landscape and climate

Mountains and **plateaus** lie in the north of Portugal, while in the south there are rolling **plains**. In the southeast there are **wetlands**. Portugal's climate is cool and rainy in the north, and warmer and drier further south.

- Parks
1. Peneda–Gerès National Park
2. Montezinho Nature Park
3. Serra da Estrela Nature Park
4. Serrras de Aire e Candeeiros Nature Park
5. Serra de São Mamede Nature Park
6. Sudoeste Alentejano e Costa Vicentina Protected Landscapes

Azores

0 100 km
0 50 miles

Madeira

0 100 km
0 50 miles

Land height above sea level:
- Over 3,250 feet
- Over 1,650 feet
- Over 650 feet
- Below 650 feet
- Country borders

River Lima
1
2 Bragança
Braga
Oporto River Douro
Caramulo Mountains
Serra del Estrela Mountains
3 ▲ Torre
Coimbra
SPAIN
PORTUGAL
Leiria
4
River Tagus
5
River Sorraira
■ **Lisbon**
Évora
Alqueva Reservoir
Setúbal Bay
Atlantic Ocean
Grândola Mountains
River Guadiana
6
Monchique Mountains
Faro
Gulf of Cádiz

0 50 100 kilometers
0 25 50 miles

N

Farming is important in the south of the country, while the north tends to be more industrial. Today around 17 percent of Portugal's land is used for **arable farming**. The main agricultural produce includes grain, potatoes, tomatoes, olives, grapes, and **cork**. Livestock is also farmed, and fishing is an important part of Portuguese life.

This map of Portugal shows the main rivers and mountains in the country.

Portugal's coastline is 1,114 miles (1,793 kilometers) long.

Mountains and lagoons

The highest Portuguese mountain is Ponta do Pico in the Azores, which is 7,713 feet (2,351 meters) high. The highest mountain on the mainland is Torre in the Serra da Estrela mountain range. It is 6,539 feet (1,993 meters) high.

The Alqueva **reservoir** is the largest reservoir in Europe, at 97 square miles (250 square kilometers). Portugal also has **lagoons**, such as Comprida Lagoon and Escura Lagoon. Both were formed from melted **glaciers** in the Serra da Estrela Mountains.

How to say...

river	*rio*	(REE-oh)
mountain	*montanha*	(mon-TAH-gna)
city	*cidade*	(see-DAH-de)
dam	*barragem*	(ba-RRA-jeim)
beach	*praia*	(PRA-yeah)
forest	*floresta*	(floo-REH-shta)

Portugal's regions

Portugal's mainland is made up of 18 districts, and its geography changes dramatically from north to south. The historic city of Oporto is found in the northern region, along with the Peneda-Gerês National Park, the Douro River, Celtic hill forts, and beautiful mountain ranges.

The central region of Portugal is home to the city of Lisbon, as well as medieval walled towns, underground caves, forests, mountains, and **vineyards**.

The southern region is made up of large plateaus, with wheat, olive trees, and cork trees. The huge Alqueva Dam and reservoir are also found here. Two mountain ranges separate the far south of Portugal from the rest of the country. This southern coastal area is well known for its popular tourist beaches, with woodlands further inland.

This map shows the 18 districts that make up Portugal. The Madiera and Azores islands are autonomous regions.

The medieval hilltop town of Óbidos is in the center of the country.

Daily life

Portugal's industry started in the north, with Oporto as the center. Northerners are often more traditional and **conservative**. The south of Portugal is a more agricultural region. There is a friendly rivalry between northerners and southerners. A saying in Oporto claims that "Lisbon has fun, Coimbra sings, Braga prays, and Oporto works." Today there are also differences between the lifestyles of rural and urban communities.

Industry and natural resources

Portuguese factories produce a range of goods. Some of the main industries include footwear and clothing manufacture, wood and cork production, paper, chemicals, metals, wine, ceramics, and telecommunications. Tourism is also a key industry.

The sea is one of Portugal's most important **natural resources**. The fishing industry has a central and historic place in the country. Other resources include cork forests, metals, marble, clay, fertile land for farming, and **hydroelectric** power. In recent years, the cultivation of cork trees for wine bottle cork stoppers has been hit hard by the widespread use of plastic and screw-top bottle stoppers.

Fishing has always been important in Portugal.

The economy

Portugal's economy has struggled to recover from decades of isolation and underdevelopment. During the 1990s, the situation improved and economic growth was above the EU average, but Portugal went into **recession** in 2008. The economy shrank by 2.6 percent in 2009, and the country faces a long, hard battle to recover. Farming and tourism are important to Portugal's economy, but both have been affected by **drought** and forest fires in recent years.

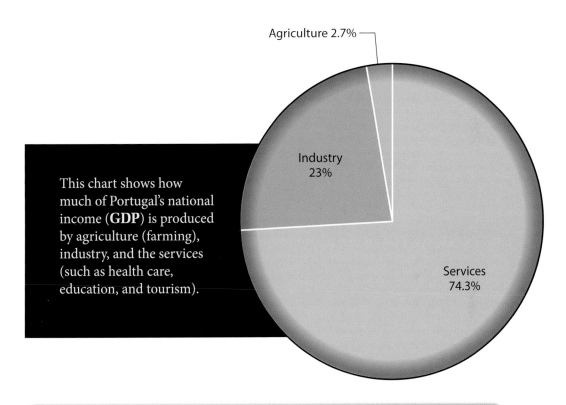

Agriculture 2.7%

Industry 23%

Services 74.3%

This chart shows how much of Portugal's national income (**GDP**) is produced by agriculture (farming), industry, and the services (such as health care, education, and tourism).

YOUNG PEOPLE

Unemployment has been a big problem for young people in Portugal. Youth unemployment increased from 11.6 percent in 2002 to 20 percent in 2009. To address this, the government plans to offer employers **incentives** to hire people younger than age 35. This could be a payment to employers for each young employee they take on.

Wildlife: Protecting the Environment

Portugal has only one national park, the Peneda-Gerês National Park in the northwest of the country. This mountainous area is wild and isolated, and many people enjoy hiking along the numerous trails within the park. The forests there are home to wild boar, wolves, and polecats, as well as birds of prey such as eagles and goshawks. There are 18 plant species in the park that are found nowhere else on the planet.

There are also more than 30 other protected natural areas in Portugal, which conserve wildlife and **habitats** in mountains, caves, **lagoons**, dunes, and marshes.

Portuguese wildlife

Some common Portuguese animals are rabbits, hares, badgers, and bats. In the right habitats deer and otters can be seen. The chameleon has been found in the Algarve since it was introduced from Africa around 70 years ago. Many birds visit Portugal during their winter **migration**, and waterbirds such as flamingos, egrets, and spoonbills can be seen in the wetland reserves of the south.

Wild boar can be found in the forests of the Peneda-Gerês National Park.

Portugal's plants

Wild orchids can be found growing in the Algarve, and in spring the wild meadows of Alentejo are covered in flowers. Vines, almonds, and citrus fruits are cultivated in the south, and **cork** oak forests are home to many species of wildlife. In the north, erica, heather, and bracken grow on heathland.

The lower sections of bark have been removed from these cork trees to make corks for bottles.

How to say...

rabbit	*coelho*	(koo-EH-lloo)
hare	*lebre*	(LE-bre)
bat	*morcego*	(mor-SEH-goo)
lynx	*lince*	(LIN-se)
wolf	*lobo*	(LOH-boo)
fish	*peixe*	(PEY- sheh)
eagle	*águia*	(A-gee-a)

Threatened species

The Iberian lynx still lives in the Malcata Mountains of the northeast, but it is seriously **endangered**. Disease, destruction of habitat, and hunting have all reduced its numbers to near extinction. **Conservationists** have set up protected areas and breeding programs to help numbers grow. The Iberian wolf is another threatened species, with only around 300 left in the wild in Portugal's northern mountains. Other endangered species include the Algarve water dog and the Spanish imperial eagle. In the seas around Madeira a nature reserve protects the rare Mediterranean monk seal.

The Iberian lynx is one of the most endangered types of cat in the world.

The environment

Environmental problems in Portugal include pollution, soil erosion, and waste disposal. The problem of **drought** is made worse by plantations of eucalyptus trees, which take in a lot of water from the ground. Dams have been built to make sure people have enough water, but the huge **reservoirs** created by the dams destroy the habitat of many species of wildlife.

Portugal is **investing** in a huge alternative energy program. The world's first commercial wave power station lies off the northern coast, there is a solar farm in Alentejo, and northern Portugal has one of Europe's largest wind farms. **Sustainable** tourism is also becoming more popular. For example, a new resort near Lisbon with accommodation for 20,000 people will damage the environment as little as possible.

Wind farms in Portugal capture the energy from winds blowing in from the Atlantic Ocean.

YOUNG PEOPLE

Children in Portugal take part in the eco-schools program, looking at ways to make their school and community more sustainable. In 2008 young people from Portugal joined pupils from Cyprus and Malta working on a project called "Tackling Climate Change in the Mediterranean Region," which won an international award.

Infrastructure: Government, Health, and Education

The Portuguese **Republic** has a type of government known as a parliamentary **democracy**. The **head of state** is a president, who is elected every five years. The leader of the government is the prime minister, who is in charge of a group of ministers appointed by the president. The Assembly of the Republic is made up of 230 elected members. The Portuguese people elect these representatives when they vote in an election, which takes place every four years.

The **currency** in Portugal is the euro. This currency, which is also used by many other countries in the **EU**, replaced the Portuguese *escudo* in 2002.

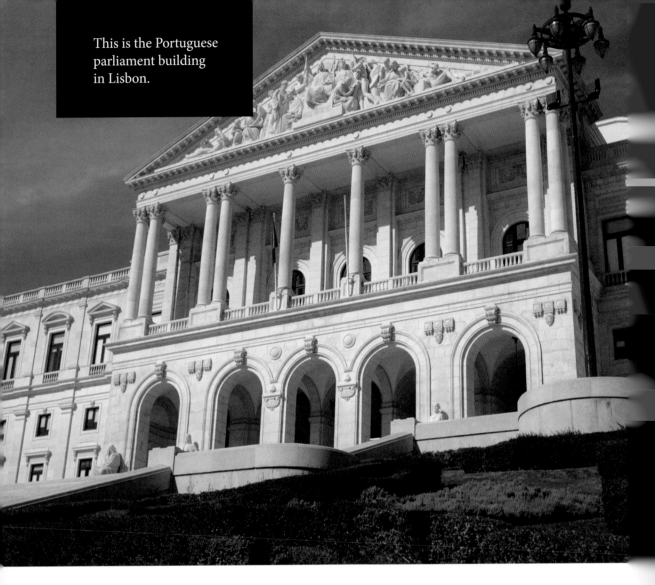

This is the Portuguese parliament building in Lisbon.

Health care

Health care is free in Portugal, including dental care. People receive good **primary health care** advice from pharmacists, reducing the number of people who need to see a doctor. Private health care is also available to those who choose to pay for it, but this is mainly in urban areas. Many hospitals in Portugal lack the most up-to-date medical technology, and waiting times for treatment can be long. Life expectancy in Portugal is 75 years for men and 82 years for women.

Education

The Portuguese government provides free education for all children in Portugal, although some families choose to pay for private education. Preschool education is optional and starts when children are three years old. There are nine years of **compulsory** school for children at primary and lower secondary school. This is followed by three years of upper secondary education for those who choose it, in preparation for college, training to do a particular job, or work. Learning foreign languages is important during all stages of education.

YOUNG PEOPLE

The school day in Portugal starts at 9:00 a.m. and finishes at 3:30 p.m., with a two-hour lunch break. Children can stay after school to join in with free activities, such as sports, music, and English. There are also breakfast clubs and after-school clubs for children whose parents work. All children have homework to do after school. Children eat a cooked meal at lunchtime consisting of three courses: soup, a main meal, and fruit. They do not have to wear a school uniform.

Time out

Children in Portugal have a summer vacation from school called *Férias Grandes* (big holidays). It lasts from late June to mid September. Grandparents often play an important role in their grandchildren's lives, since in many families both parents work and need help during the summer. There are also shorter school holidays at Christmas, during *Carnaval* in February, and at Easter.

These children are attending a math lesson in Sacavém, near Lisbon.

How to say...

school	*escola*	(sh-Ko-la)
teacher	*professo*	(pru-FE-sor)
timetable	*horário*	(or-A-ryo)
homework	*dever de casa*	(dver-de-KA-za)
holiday	*ferias*	(FAIR-ee-ash)
university	*universidade*	(oo-ni-vers-i-DA-d)

Culture: *Fado*, Family, and Fun

The Portuguese people have a strong sense of national **identity**, which is reflected in a unique **culture**. Some traditions remain stronger in the countryside, while urban areas have taken in some cultural aspects of **immigrant** communities from Africa and Brazil.

Music

Fado is Portugal's most famous music. This is a type of folk music, involving singing, a twelve-string Portuguese guitar, and an instrument called a viola, which is actually a six-string Spanish guitar. Amália Rodrigues was one of the most famous *fado* singers. Carlos Paredes and António Chainho are two well-known Portuguese guitar players.

Other popular music in Portugal includes jazz, African-influenced music, and rock. David Fonseca is a well-known pop singer who often performs in English.

The twelve-string Portuguese guitar makes a beautiful accompaniment to *fado* singing.

AMÁLIA RODRIGUES (1920–1999)

Amália Rodrigues grew up in Lisbon with her grandmother. She became known as the "Queen of Fado" and helped to make the music famous around the world. Many gifted composers and poets wrote music and words especially for her to sing. When she died there were three days of official **mourning** in Portugal.

Visual art

The 16th-century painters Vasco Fernandes and Gaspar Vaz are famous for their religious art. In the 17th century the female artist Josefa de Óbidos produced still-life paintings as well as religious artworks. Her paintings are full of strong color and detail. Paula Rego is an artist who left Portugal when Salazar was in power. Her paintings often have a fantasy style and use bold color. Helena Almeida is a photographer who is well known for her unusual portraits.

The artist Paula Rego is famous for her art, which depicts reality alongside fantasy.

Sports

Soccer (what they call football) is very important in Portugal. In 2004 the country hosted the European Football (Soccer) Championships, and the Portuguese team reached the final, where they were defeated by Greece. Many talented Portuguese soccer players play for the best clubs in the world. Perhaps the biggest soccer star is Christiano Ronaldo, who plays for Real Madrid in Spain. Lisbon (with Sporting Lisbon and Benfica) and Oporto have Portugal's strongest home teams.

Soccer star Cristiano Ronaldo was born on the Portuguese island of Madeira.

Other popular sports in Portugal are basketball, swimming, athletics, tennis, and cycling. Olympic athletes include triple jumper Nelson Évora and the marathon runner Rosa Mota. Many people watch motor racing at Estoril, and young people enjoy surfing on the Atlantic coast. Bullfighting also takes place in Portugal, but today many people strongly oppose this sport for animal welfare reasons.

NELSON ÉVORA (BORN 1984)

Nelson Évora was born in the Ivory Coast and moved to Portugal when he was a child. He started competing for Portugal in 2002, when he became a Portuguese citizen. Évora was world champion in the triple jump in 2007 and then won gold at the 2008 Olympics in Beijing. He has also competed in long jump and high jump competitions.

Books

Luís Vaz de Camões is the most famous Portuguese author. He was a 16th-century poet who wrote *The Lusíadas*, an epic poem about the discovery of the New World. During Salazar's oppressive regime many writers and artists were prevented from expressing themselves freely, but in 1998 the Nobel Prize for Literature was awarded to the author José Saramago. He wrote powerful and controversial books about religion and human nature. António Lobo Antunes writes historical novels with an edge of fantasy, while Sophia de Mello Breyner Andresen was a prize-winning poet who also wrote children's books.

Traditions and customs

Portuguese people tend to be polite and traditional. Strangers meet with a handshake. Female friends kiss twice on the cheek, and male friends often meet with a handshake and hug. People normally bring a gift when visiting someone's home.

Festivals

Religious festivals are important in Portugal. At Christmas, families give gifts on Christmas Eve, and on New Year's Eve people eat 12 grapes as the clock strikes midnight. This is to ensure 12 happy months ahead or to have 12 wishes.

During *Carnaval* in February or March, children parade along village streets in costumes, and adults enjoy *Carnaval* parties. All Souls Day on November 2 or 3 is celebrated by children going from door to door asking for *pão por Deus* (bread for God's sake)—they are given sweets.

Food

Most families share daily meals. Different Portuguese regions have their own food specialities. Salted cod and other fish, such as sardines, are very popular, as are meaty stews, grilled chicken, and spicy *piri-piri* sauce. Meals are usually served with rice, potatoes, and salad. Portuguese cakes include custard tarts called *pastéis de nata* and cakes made from carrots, beans, and pumpkin.

How to say...

salted cod	*bacalhau*	(ba-KA-llau)
chicken	*frango*	(FRAN-goo)
ice cream	*gelado*	(je-LAH-doo)
cake	*bolo*	(BO-loo)

Portuguese rice pudding

This delicious traditional dessert is often decorated with cinnamon in fancy shapes and patterns. Ask an adult to help you.

Ingredients

- 3 cups milk
- 1 cup long-grain rice
- 1 cup sugar
- zest of 3 or 4 unwaxed lemons
- 3 egg yolks
- a small pinch of salt
- ground cinnamon

What to do

1. Bring the milk, rice, and sugar to a boil over a gentle heat. Add the lemon zest when the mixture begins to bubble.
2. Let it cook over a low heat for 20 minutes.
3. Remove the rice from the heat and add the egg yolks and salt.
4. Return the mixture to a very low heat and stir while the egg yolks cook.
5. Pour into a shallow dish and decorate with the ground cinnamon when cool. Serve hot or cold.

Portugal Today

Over the centuries many Portuguese people have **emigrated** to live in other countries in Europe and around the world. Today there are large Portuguese communities in the United States, France, Germany, and Brazil. Meanwhile a growing number of **immigrants** are settling in Portugal, particularly in the cities of Oporto and Lisbon, and in the south. Alongside these changes, many young people are moving to the cities from the countryside, creating a divide between aging rural communities and younger urban populations.

Many young people are attracted by Portugal's bustling capital city, Lisbon.

The biggest problem facing the Portuguese people is the state of their **economy**. By 2011, Portugal's government had record debts, and this resulted in huge spending cuts that have hit ordinary people hard. **Unemployment** is high, particularly among young people, and tough challenges lie ahead.

Despite these issues, Portugal's people remain very proud of their country and **culture**. The tourism industry continues to grow as more and more people discover the country's beautiful scenery and the historic towns beyond the beaches of the south. Portuguese figures such as Cristiano Ronaldo, José Barroso, and Paula Rego are known internationally. Portugal has survived difficult times throughout its history, and its people are resilient enough to cope with the challenges of the future.

Portugal's dramatic Atlantic coastline is popular with surfers from around the world.

Fact File

Official long name:	Portuguese Republic
Official language:	Portuguese
Capital city:	Lisbon
Bordering country:	Spain
Currency:	euro
Population:	10,760,300 (2011 estimate)
Percentage of population living in urban areas:	61 percent
Percentage of population living in rural areas:	39 percent
Birth rate:	9.94 births per 1,000 people
Life expectancy (total):	78.54 years
Life expectancy (men):	75.28 years
Life expectancy (women):	82.01 years
number of internet users:	5,168,800 (48 percent of the population)
Type of government:	parliamentary democracy
National flower:	lavender
Climate:	maritime temperate
Area (total):	35,556 square miles (92,090 square kilometers)
Highest point:	Ponta do Pico in the Azores—7,713 feet (2,351 meters)
Lowest point:	Atlantic Ocean—0 feet/meters
Natural resources:	fish, forests (cork), iron ore, copper, zinc, tin, tungsten, silver, gold, uranium, marble, clay, gypsum, salt, arable land, hydropower

Major industries:	textiles, clothing, footwear, wood and cork, paper, chemicals, auto-parts manufacturing, base metals, dairy products, wine and other foods, porcelain and ceramics, glassware, technology, telecommunications, ship construction and refurbishment, tourism
Agricultural produce:	grain, potatoes, tomatoes, olives, grapes, sheep, cattle, goats, pigs, poultry, dairy products, fish
Exports:	agricultural products, food products, oil products, chemical products, plastics and rubber, skins and leather, wood and cork, wood pulp and paper, textile materials, clothing, footwear, minerals and mineral products, base metals, machinery and tools, vehicles and other transportation materials, optical and precision instruments
Famous Portuguese people :	Bartolomeu Dias (explorer, c. 1451–1500) Vasco da Gama (explorer, c. 1460–1524) Maria de Lourdes Pintassilgo (2nd female prime minister in Europe, 1930–2004) José Manuel Durão Barroso (president of the European Commission, born 1956) Amália Rodrigues (*fado* singer, 1920–1999) Carlos Paredes (musician, 1925–2004) António Chainho (musician, born 1938) Josefa de Óbidos (artist, 1630–1684) Paula Rego (artist, born 1935) José Saramago (writer, 1922–2010) António Lobo Antunes (writer, born 1942) Luís Figo (soccer player, born 1972) Cristiano Ronaldo (soccer player, born 1985) Nelson Évora (athlete, born 1984) Rosa Mota (athlete, born 1958)

National Holidays: January 1—New Year's Day
February/March—Carnaval Tuesday
March/April—Good Friday and Easter Day
April 25—Liberty Day
May 1—International Labor Day
June 10—Portugal Day
August 15—Feast of the Assumption
October 5—Republic Day
November 1— All Saints Day
December 1—Independence Day
December 8—Feast of the Immaculate Conception
December 25—Christmas Day

Portugal's national anthem

This is a translation of *A Portuguesa* (The Portuguese Song):

Heroes of the sea, noble race,
Valiant and immortal nation,
Rise up once again
The splendour of Portugal.
Out of the mists of memory,
Oh Homeland, we hear the voices
Of your great forefathers
That shall lead you on to victory!

The chance to see dolphins in the wild attracts visitors to the beautiful Portuguese islands of the Azores.

Timeline

22,000 years ago	Early humans paint art on rocks in northwest Portugal
5,500 BCE	Hilltop towns and villages are established around northern Portugal
700 BCE	**Celts** begin to arrive in northern Portugal
210 BCE	Romans begin to move into the south and east of Portugal
139 BCE	The warrior Viriathus dies
60 BCE	Romans establish a capital at Olisipo (Lisbon)
406 CE	The Roman **Empire** begins to decline, and the Suevi **tribe** from Germany settles in the north
469 CE	Visigoths invade northern Portugal
711 CE	**Moors** settle on the southern coast
718 CE	Christian *Reconquista* of lands held by the Moors begins
1139	Afonso I becomes first king of Portugal
1297	Last Portuguese territory taken from the Moors
1415	Prince Henry the Navigator starts to encourage explorers to discover new land
1419	Portuguese explorers arrive in Madeira
1427	Portuguese explorers arrive in the Azores
1488	Bartolomeu Dias sails round the southern tip of Africa

1500	The Portuguese explorer Pedro Álvares Cabral arrives in Brazil
1580	King Felipe II of Spain is crowned King Felipe I of Portugal
1640	The Spanish governor of Portugal is removed and the Duke of Bragança becomes King João IV
1755	Earthquakes destroy Lisbon
1807	Napoleon invades Portugal
1811	Napoleon is driven out of Portugal
1822	Brazil becomes **independent**
1890	Many Portuguese people **emigrate** to Brazil
1908	King Dom Carlos and his son are **assassinated**
1910	Portugal is declared a **republic**
1932	António de Oliviera Salazar becomes prime minister
1970	Salazar dies
1974	Revolution of the Carnations takes place. Most Portuguese colonies start to gain independence.
1979	Maria de Lourdes Pintassilgo becomes prime minister
1986	Portugal joins the **European Union (EU)**
1992	Trade barriers with the rest of the EU are removed
2004	José Manuel Durão Barroso becomes Portugal's first president of the **European Commission**. Portugal hosts the European Football (Soccer) Championships.
2005	José Sócrates becomes prime minister
2008	Global financial crisis hits Portugal's **economy** hard

Glossary

ally person, group, or country that is united with another

arable farming growing of crops

assassinate kill someone for political reasons

Celts groups of people who lived across Europe from 750 BCE

Christianity religion based on the teachings of Jesus Christ

civil war war between people of the same country

coalition government made up of two or more political parties

colony country or area that has been settled in by people from another country

compulsory required or demanded

conservative traditional, against rapid change

conservationist person who works to look after something for the future. Animal conservationists try to protect endagered species from dying out.

cork very light, soft wood that comes from the bark of a cork oak tree

coup sudden overthrow of government

culture practices, traditions, and beliefs of a society

currency banknotes and coins accepted in exchange for goods and services

democracy government of a country elected by its own people

drought long period of time without rain

economy relating to the money, industry, and jobs in a country

emigrate move to and settle in another country

empire group of countries ruled by a single government or ruler

endangered threatened with dying out

European Commission organization within the EU that deals with laws, treaties, and the running of the EU

European Union (EU) international organization of European countries with shared political and economic aims. The EU formed in 1993 from the EEC (European Economic Community).

fortress strong building that is used to defend a town, such a castle

GDP Gross Domestic Product; the value of goods and services produced by a country within one year

glacier large mass of moving ice

habitat environment where a plant or animal is found

head of state main public representative of a country, such as a queen or president

hydroelectric relating to electricity produced by flowing water

identity characteristics by which a person or thing is known

immigrant person who has moved to another country and settled there

incentive something that encourages people to do something

independent not ruled or controlled by another country or people

infrastructure organizations and facilities

invest put money into a business in order to develop that business and make more money in the future

Jew person who is a member of the Jewish race or religion

lagoon body of salt water that is separated from the sea

legacy things that are handed down or left to the next generation

migration permanent movement of people to a new country or region

monarchy government led by a king or queen

Moor person from the mainly Arab countries in northwest Africa

mourn feel deep sadness over the loss of something

Muslim person who follows the religion of Islam, based on the teachings of Muhammad

natural resource raw material found in nature

Neolithic latest part of the Stone Age

plain large, flat area of land

plateau large, flat area of high land

primary health care essential health care and information available in the community

recession period of economic decline

refugee person who has escaped from his or her home or country because of a war or disaster

republic country without a king or queen, usually with a single, elected leader

reservoir place where water is stored

settler person who moves to a new area and stays there

socialist someone who believes that a country's main industries should be owned by the government, not by individual people

sustainable use of resources that does not damage the environment and will also be available in the future

tax money paid by people to the government. Taxes can come from wages or be placed on goods that people buy.

tribe independent social group, historically often made up of primitive or nomadic people

tsunami huge, destructive sea wave caused by an earthquake or volcano

unemployment situation where a person has no paid work

vineyard area where grapes are farmed for wine production

wetland marshy land

Find Out More

Books

Ariganello, Lisa. *Henry the Navigator: Prince of Portuguese Exploration.* New York: Crabtree Publishing, 2006.

Bailey, Katharine. *Vasco Da Gama: Quest for the Spice Trade.* New York: Crabtree Publishing, 2007.

Deckker, Zilah. *Portugal.* Washington, DC: National Geographic Children's Books, 2009.

Etingoff, Kim. *Portugal.* Broomall, PA: Mason Crest, 2005.

Marcelino, Pedro, and Slawko Waschuk. *Junior Jetsetters Guide to Lisbon.* Toronto: Junior Jetsetters Inc., 2010.

DVDs

The Best of Portugal. Tampa, FL: TravelVideoStore.com, 2008.

Megan McCormick. *Globe Trekker: Portugal & the Azores.* Directed by Ian Cross. Los Angeles, CA: 555 Productions, 2004.

Rick Steves' Europe: Spain & Portugal 2000–2009. New York: Perseus, 2009.

Websites

www.cia.gov/library/publications/the-world-factbook/geos/ts.html

The World Factbook is a publication of the Central Intelligence Agency (CIA) of the United States. It provides information on the history, people, government, economy, geography, communications, transportation, and military of Portugal and over 250 other countries.

http://www.lonelyplanet.com/portugal

The Lonely Planet website offers some introductory information about Portugal, its history and culture, and some favorite destinations.

www.visitportugal.com

Portugal's official tourist website has information about the regions, foods, and history of the country.

Places to visit

If you ever get the chance to go to Portugal, here are some interesting places to visit:

Oceanário des Lisboa (Oceanarium)

Parque das Nações, Lisbon

www.oceanario.pt

This huge aquarium has 450 different species of sea life for you to watch underwater.

Serra do Gerês protected reserve

This nature reserve in the north of the country is a great place to visit for hiking, water sports, and camping.

Castelo de Säo Jorge (St. George's Castle)

Largo do Chao da Feira, Lisbon

Visit the castle for the best views across the city.

Beaches on the Atlantic coast

Portugal has a long and beautiful coastline. Try bodyboarding and surfing on the waves.

Museu do Fado (Museum of Fado)

Lisbon

www.museudofado.pt

Hear and learn more about Portugal's unique Fado music and its history at this Lisbon museum.

Topic Tools

You can use these topic tools for your school projects. Trace the map onto a sheet of paper, using the black outline to guide you.

The shields and castles on Portugal's flag represent the defeat of the Moors. The globe shows the discoveries made by Portuguese explorers. The color green represents hope for the future, and red is for the blood of Portugal's heroes. Copy the flag design and then color in your picture. Make sure you use the right colors!

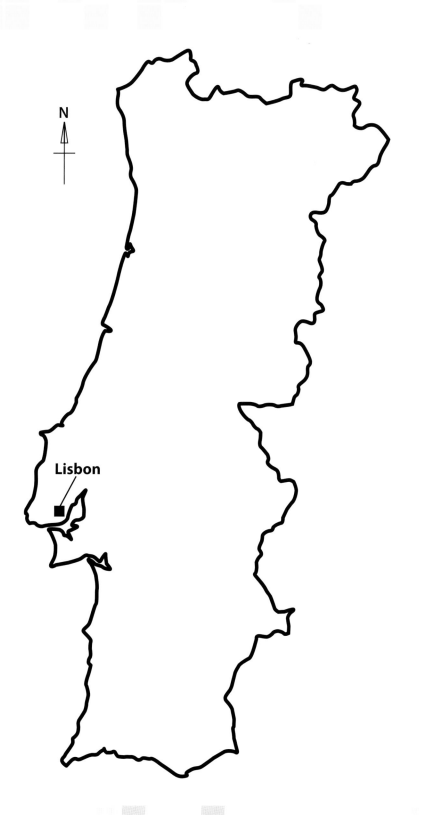

N

Lisbon

Index

Titles in the series

Afghanistan	978 1 4329 5195 5	Japan	978 1 4329 6102 2
Algeria	978 1 4329 6093 3	Latvia	978 1 4329 5211 2
Australia	978 1 4329 6094 0	Liberia	978 1 4329 6103 9
Brazil	978 1 4329 5196 2	Libya	978 1 4329 6104 6
Canada	978 1 4329 6095 7	Lithuania	978 1 4329 5212 9
Chile	978 1 4329 5197 9	Mexico	978 1 4329 5213 6
China	978 1 4329 6096 4	Morocco	978 1 4329 6105 3
Costa Rica	978 1 4329 5198 6	New Zealand	978 1 4329 6106 0
Cuba	978 1 4329 5199 3	North Korea	978 1 4329 6107 7
Czech Republic	978 1 4329 5200 6	Pakistan	978 1 4329 5214 3
Egypt	978 1 4329 6097 1	Philippines	978 1 4329 6108 4
England	978 1 4329 5201 3	Poland	978 1 4329 5215 0
Estonia	978 1 4329 5202 0	Portugal	978 1 4329 6109 1
France	978 1 4329 5203 7	Russia	978 1 4329 6110 7
Germany	978 1 4329 5204 4	Scotland	978 1 4329 5216 7
Greece	978 1 4329 6098 8	South Africa	978 1 4329 6112 1
Haiti	978 1 4329 5205 1	South Korea	978 1 4329 6113 8
Hungary	978 1 4329 5206 8	Spain	978 1 4329 6111 4
Iceland	978 1 4329 6099 5	Tunisia	978 1 4329 6114 5
India	978 1 4329 5207 5	United States of America	978 1 4329 6115 2
Iran	978 1 4329 5208 2	Vietnam	978 1 4329 6116 9
Iraq	978 1 4329 5209 9	Wales	978 1 4329 5217 4
Ireland	978 1 4329 6100 8	Yemen	978 1 4329 5218 1
Israel	978 1 4329 6101 5		
Italy	978 1 4329 5210 5		